D0579128

AMAZING BASEBALL RECORDS

BY BRIAN HOWELL

The Child's World

Published by The Child's World®
1980 Lookout Drive • Mankato, MN 56003-1705
800-599-READ • www.childsworld.com

Acknowledgments
The Child's World®: Mary Berendes, Publishing Director
Red Line Editorial: Editorial direction
The Design Lab: Design
Amnet: Production

Design Element: Shutterstock Images

Photographs ©: Greg Trott/AP Images, Cover; Library
of Congress, 5, 15; Bettmann/Corbis/AP Images, 7;
Eric Risberg/AP Images, 9; AP Images, 11, 29; Paul
Sakuma/AP Images, 13; Ed Kolenovsky/AP Images, 17;
Anthony Correia/Shutterstock Images, 19; Elise
Amendola/AP Images, 21; Mark J. Terrill/AP Images, 23;
Sporting News/Getty Images, 25; Sports Illustrated/
Getty Images, 27

ISBN 9781614734017
LCCN 2012946496

Printed in the United States of America
Mankato, MN
November, 2012
PA02146

Disclaimer: The information in this book is current
through the 2012 MLB season.

ABOUT THE AUTHOR
Brian Howell is a freelance writer
from Denver, Colorado. He has
been a sports journalist for nearly
20 years, writing about high
school, college, and professional
sports. He has also written books
about sports and history.

TABLE OF CONTENTS

CHAPTER ONE

The Game of Baseball . . . 4

CHAPTER TWO

Amazing Offensive Records . . . 8

CHAPTER THREE

Amazing Pitching Records . . . 14

CHAPTER FOUR

Amazing Baseball Teams . . . 20

CHAPTER FIVE

Other Amazing Baseball Records . . . 24

Glossary . . . 30

Learn More . . . 31

Index . . . 32

THE GAME OF BASEBALL

Professional baseball has been played in the United States since the middle of the 1800s. The game has changed a little over the years. Some of the rules today are different than they were in the 1800s. But the game is very much the same as it was in 1869. That's the year that the Cincinnati Red Stockings became the first professional baseball team. From that time on, there have been some amazing baseball players making and breaking great records.

One of the most amazing baseball records was made during the summer of 1941 by Joe DiMaggio of the New York Yankees. Just 26 years old, DiMaggio was already a five-time All-Star. He was also the American League's (AL) Most Valuable Player in 1939.

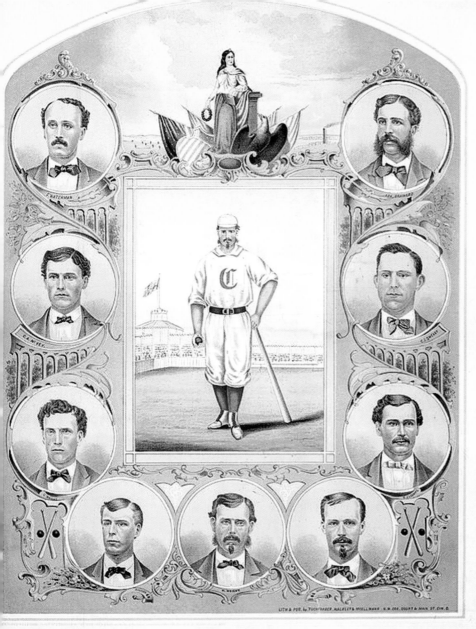

FIRST NINE OF THE

CINCINNATI
(RED STOCKINGS) BASE BALL CLUB.

THE IRON MAN

Cal Ripken Jr. of the Baltimore Orioles played in a stunning 2,632 consecutive games from May 30, 1982, to September 19, 1998. He broke what was once thought to be an unbreakable record of 2,130 consecutive games. That was set by Lou Gehrig of the New York Yankees from June 1, 1925, to April 30, 1939.

A poster shows the 1869 Cincinnati Red Stockings, the first professional baseball team in the United States.

From May 15 to July 16, 1941, DiMaggio got on base with a hit in 56 consecutive games. He broke the record of 45 set by Willie Keeler in the 1896 and 1897 seasons. DiMaggio's **streak** started with one base hit on May 15 against the Chicago White Sox. During his 56-game streak, DiMaggio had 91 hits, including 15 home runs. On July 17, the Cleveland Indians finally put an end to the streak. DiMaggio went to the plate four times and failed to get a hit. The next day he began a 16-game hitting streak.

DiMaggio is still remembered best for his hitting streak. As of 2012, his 56-game hitting streak was still a major league record. Since DiMaggio's streak, the longest streak in the majors has been 44 games, by Pete Rose in 1978. Only five players have managed streaks of at least 35 games since 1941.

SCORELESS STREAK

In 1988, pitcher Orel Hershiser of the Los Angeles Dodgers had a season to remember. He had 23 wins and 8 losses. He won the Cy Young Award, which is given each year to the best pitcher in the AL and National League (NL). He also helped the Dodgers win the World Series. He had a remarkable streak of 59 consecutive scoreless innings pitched. He broke the record of 58 2/3 set by former Dodger Don Drysdale in 1968.

LONGEST HITTING STREAKS
Joe DiMaggio's streak in 1941 is one of Major League Baseball's (MLB) greatest records. The longest streak by a college player is 60 games. It was set by Damian Costantino of Division III Salve Regina University from 2001 to 2003. The longest Division I college streak was 58 games by Robin Ventura of Oklahoma State in 1987.

Joe DiMaggio takes a swing during game 53 of his 56-game streak on July 13, 1941.

AMAZING OFFENSIVE RECORDS

Two of baseball's most famous records are home runs in a single season and home runs in a career. One man holds both of these records.

In 2001, Barry Bonds of the San Francisco Giants hit an amazing 73 home runs to set a new single-season record. Then he took aim at Hank Aaron's career mark of 755 home runs. On August 7, 2007, Bonds hit the 756th home run of his career. He became the new home-run king. He would hit six more before finishing his career with a total of 762 home runs.

PLAYERS WITH 60 OR MORE HOME RUNS IN A SINGLE SEASON

PLAYER	HOME RUNS	SEASON
Barry Bonds	73	2001
Mark McGwire	70	1998
Sammy Sosa	66	1998
Mark McGwire	65	1999
Sammy Sosa	63	1999
Roger Maris	61	1961
Babe Ruth	60	1927

WORLD SERIES RECORD

During Game 3 of the 2011 World Series, St. Louis Cardinals slugger Albert Pujols had one of the most remarkable games in Series history. Pujols tied World Series single-game records for home runs (3), runs scored (4), hits (5), and runs batted in (6). He is the only player to reach all of those numbers in the same World Series game.

Barry Bonds celebrates after hitting his 756th home run on August 7, 2007.

ALL-TIME HOME-RUN LEADERS (CAREER)

1. Barry Bonds: 762
2. Hank Aaron: 755
3. Babe Ruth: 714
4. Willie Mays: 660
5. Alex Rodriguez*: 647

*Active as of 2012

GREATEST HITS

Pete Rose had 4,256 hits during his career. That is more than any other player in history. Rose was a switch-hitter who played from 1963 to 1986. A switch-hitter is someone who can hit from both sides of the plate. He used that to his advantage during his career, in which he played for the Cincinnati Reds, Philadelphia Phillies, and Montreal Expos. A 17-time All-Star, Rose led the National League in hits in seven different seasons.

MOST HITS IN A SINGLE SEASON

PLAYER	HITS	SEASON
Ichiro Suzuki	262	2004
George Sisler	257	1920
Lefty O'Doul	254	1929
Bill Terry	254	1930
Al Simmons	253	1925

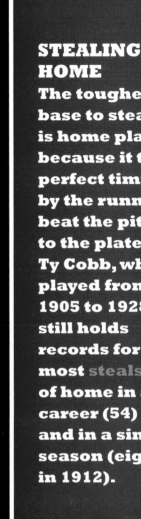

STEALING HOME

The toughest base to steal is home plate, because it takes perfect timing by the runner to beat the pitch to the plate. Ty Cobb, who played from 1905 to 1928, still holds records for most steals of home in a career (54) and in a single season (eight in 1912).

Pete Rose of the Cincinnati Reds bats against the Atlanta Braves in a game on August 2, 1978.

ALL-TIME HIT LEADERS (CAREER)

1. Pete Rose: 4,256
2. Ty Cobb: 4,189
3. Hank Aaron: 3,771
4. Stan Musial: 3,630
5. Tris Speaker: 3,514

BEST BASE STEALER

Rickey Henderson played for nine different teams during a career that started in 1979 and ended in 2003. During his career, he stole 1,406 bases. That is by far the most in baseball history. Henderson had a single-season record of 130 steals in 1982.

Henderson's stolen-base records are probably safe for awhile. Through 2012, no player was within 800 steals of Henderson's total. Also, no player has swiped more than 80 bases in a season since 1988. That is when Henderson stole 93 bases and Vince Coleman stole 81.

ALL-TIME STOLEN-BASE LEADERS (CAREER)
1. Rickey Henderson: 1,406
2. Lou Brock: 938
3. Billy Hamilton: 914
4. Ty Cobb: 897
5. Tim Raines: 808

COLEMAN'S STEAL STREAK
From September 18, 1988, to July 26, 1989,
Vince Coleman of the St. Louis Cardinals
could not be stopped. He was successful on
50 consecutive steal attempts. That is the
best streak in history. Coleman led the NL in
steals during each of his first six seasons.

Rickey Henderson
steals a base on
August 24, 1982.

THREE

AMAZING PITCHING
RECORDS

During Cy Young's era (1890–1911) starting pitchers pitched more often and stayed in the game longer than they do now. Because of that, nobody in today's game will likely ever touch Young's records. What made Young remarkable, though, is that nobody in his day could touch them, either. He is the all-time leader in wins (511), games started (815), completed games (749), and innings pitched (7,356). Baseball began recognizing the best pitcher each season in 1956. It is no wonder that honor became known as the Cy Young Award.

RECORDS MADE TO LAST

Charles "Old Hoss" Radbourn won 59 games in 1884, still the most in any season. Jack Chesbro had 41 wins in 1904, the most by any pitcher since 1900. Both records seem pretty safe. Since 1934, only one pitcher has had more than 30 wins in a season. Denny McLain of the Detroit Tigers had 31 wins in 1968.

Cy Young throws a baseball in 1908.

ALL-TIME WINS LEADERS (CAREER)

1. Cy Young: 511
2. Walter Johnson: 417
3. Pete Alexander: 373
   Christy Mathewson: 373
5. Pud Galvin: 365

ONE, TWO, THREE STRIKES YOU'RE OUT!

Very few pitchers in baseball history were as good at striking out hitters as Nolan Ryan. The "Ryan Express" played 27 years (1966–1993)—more than any other player. He set the all-time **strikeout** record with 5,714. Ryan led the American League in strikeouts nine times and led the National League twice. He also won 324 games and pitched more **no-hitters** (seven) than any pitcher in history.

MOST STRIKEOUTS IN A SEASON (SINCE 1900)

PLAYER	STRIKEOUTS	SEASON
Nolan Ryan	383	1973
Sandy Koufax	382	1965
Randy Johnson	372	2001
Nolan Ryan	367	1974
Randy Johnson	364	1999

KNOCKING OUT 20

Only three times in baseball history has a pitcher struck out at least 20 hitters in a game. Roger Clemens did so twice: on April 29, 1986, and September 18, 1996. Kerry Wood did it on May 6, 1998. They are the only two who did so in a nine-inning game.

Houston Astros pitcher Nolan Ryan hurls the ball on September 26, 1981, against the Los Angeles Dodgers at the Houston Astrodome.

ALL-TIME STRIKEOUT LEADERS (CAREER)

1. Nolan Ryan: 5,714
2. Randy Johnson: 4,875
3. Roger Clemens: 4,672
4. Steve Carlton: 4,136
5. Bert Blyleven: 3,701

CLOSING THEM OUT

During the last several decades, the need for quality relief pitchers has increased in baseball. A relief pitcher is any pitcher who did not start the game for his team. Mariano Rivera has been the best at closing out games. From 1995 to 2012, Rivera notched a whopping 608 saves for the New York Yankees. Saves are when a pitcher comes into a close game that his team is leading, and he finishes off the win.

Mariano Rivera of the New York Yankees pitches against the New York Mets on May 20, 2006.

MOST SAVES IN A SEASON

PLAYER	SAVES	SEASON
Francisco Rodriguez	62	2008
Bobby Thigpen	57	1990
Eric Gagne	55	2003
John Smoltz	55	2002
Trevor Hoffman	53	1998
Randy Myers	53	1993
Mariano Rivera	53	2004

ALONE AT THE TOP
John Smoltz is the only pitcher in baseball history with at least 200 wins and more than 150 saves. He had 213 wins and 154 saves in 21 seasons. He played all but one of those with the Atlanta Braves.

ALL-TIME SAVES LEADERS (CAREER)
1. Mariano Rivera: 608*
2. Trevor Hoffman: 601
3. Lee Smith: 478
4. John Franco: 424
5. Billy Wagner: 422

*Active as of 2012

FOUR

AMAZING BASEBALL TEAMS

In 2009, the New York Yankees won their 40th AL championship, or **pennant**. In the same year, they won their 27th World Series title. Those numbers are, by far, the most of any team in history.

BLUE JAYS POUND THE BALL

On September 14, 1987, the Toronto Blue Jays hit a whopping ten home runs during an 18–3 win over the Baltimore Orioles. They became the only team to hit ten in a game. Catcher Ernie Whitt smacked three of the Blue Jays' home runs that night.

MOST PENNANTS WON

TEAM	PENNANTS WON
New York Yankees	40
Brooklyn/Los Angeles Dodgers	22
St. Louis Cardinals	22
New York/San Francisco Giants	22
Boston/Milwaukee/Atlanta Braves	17

SOX AND SOX FINISH ON TOP

In 2004, the Boston Red Sox won the World Series for the first time since 1918. The next season, the Chicago White Sox won the Series for the first time since 1917.

New York Yankees' Jerry Hairston Jr. (17) celebrates with teammates after scoring during Game 2 of the AL Championship Series on October 18, 2009.

MOST WORLD SERIES VICTORIES

1. New York Yankees: 27
2. St. Louis Cardinals: 11
3. Philadelphia/Kansas City/Oakland Athletics: 9
4. Boston Red Sox: 7
   New York/San Francisco Giants: 7

CONSISTENT WINNERS

Throughout the history of baseball, no team has won more games than the New York/San Francisco Giants. Through the 2012 season, the Giants had won 10,616 games. The Giants had been to the **postseason** 24 times since 1883. There are 55 Giants players that are in the Hall of Fame. That is the most of any team.

BRAVES REACH 10K AND 10K
Through the 2012 season, the Atlanta Braves were the only baseball team with at least 10,000 wins (10,128) and 10,000 losses (10,095).

San Francisco Giants teammates congratulate Brandon Belt (left) after he hit a home run on April 1, 2011.

MOST WINS IN A SEASON

TEAM	WINS–LOSSES	SEASON
Chicago Cubs	116–36	1906
Seattle Mariners	116–46	2001
New York Yankees	114–48	1998
Cleveland Indians	111–43	1954
Pittsburgh Pirates	110–42	1909
New York Yankees	110–44	1927

LONG BALL

The Seattle Mariners hit home runs at a historic rate in 1997. The Mariners finished with a major league record of 264 home runs that season. Ken Griffey Jr. hit 56 of those home runs. Jay Buhner had 40 home runs. Six players had at least 20 home runs.

LONGEST WINNING STREAKS

1. New York Giants: 26 wins in 1916*
2. Chicago White Stockings: 21 wins in 1880
3. Chicago Cubs: 21 wins in 1935
4. Oakland Athletics: 20 wins in 2002

*Streak included one tie

FIVE

OTHER AMAZING BASEBALL RECORDS

On May 1, 1920, the Boston Braves and Brooklyn Robins played a historic game. Squaring off at Braves Field, the two teams played 26 innings. It is still the longest game in major league history. Not even 26 innings could decide the outcome, though. The game ended in a 1–1 tie. Brooklyn's Leon Cadore and Boston's Joe Oeschger both pitched all 26 innings.

MOST TEAMS PLAYED FOR

PLAYER	YEARS	NUMBER OF TEAMS
Octavio Dotel*	1999–2012	13
Deacon McGuire	1884–1912	12
Mike Morgan	1978–2002	12
Matt Stairs	1992–2011	12
Ron Villone	1995–2009	12

*Active as of 2012

HOMER HIGH STREAKS TO 75
From 2004 to 2005, Homer High School in Michigan had a 75-game winning streak. That is the longest streak ever for a high school, college, or pro team.

Pitcher Leon Cadore shares an MLB record with Joe Oeschger for the most innings pitched in a single game.

PACIOREK'S GAME TO REMEMBER

John Paciorek is one of 27 players to post a 1.000 (perfect) batting average for his career, but he's the only one to do it with at least three major league at-bats. On September 29, 1963, Paciorek, who was 18 years old, played in his only major league game, for the Houston Colt .45s. He went 3-for-3 with four runs scored, three RBIs, and two walks in his five plate appearances. He spent five more years in the minor leagues but never again reached the majors.

MOST WINS BY A MANAGER (CAREER)

MANAGER	WINS
Connie Mack (1894–1950)	3,731
John McGraw (1899–1932)	2,763
Tony La Russa (1979–2011)	2,728
Bobby Cox (1978–2010)	2,504
Joe Torre (1977–2010)	2,326

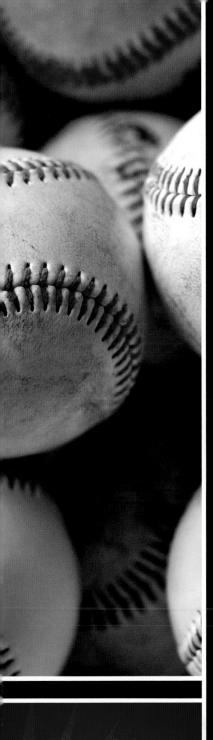

John Paciorek, who later became a teacher and coach, holds a perfect batting average for his major league career.

REGGIE BLASTS THREE HOMERS

On October 18, 1977, Reggie Jackson of the
New York Yankees had one of the most amazing World
Series games of all time. He hit three home runs during
Game 6 of the World Series, and he did it on three
consecutive pitches. Through 2012, Jackson was one
of only four players to smack three homers in a World
Series game. Babe Ruth did it twice, in 1926 and
1928. Albert Pujols accomplished the feat in 2011,
and Pablo Sandoval did it in 2012.

ONE STRIKE FROM DEFEAT

Only two teams in major league history have been one strike away from losing the World Series and then come back to win it: the 1986 New York Mets (against the Boston Red Sox) and the 2011 St. Louis Cardinals (against the Texas Rangers). The Cardinals were one strike away from defeat twice before pulling off the Series win.

Reggie Jackson hits the second of three home runs in Game 6 of the 1977 World Series.

GLOSSARY

consecutive (kuhn-SEK-yuh-tiv): Something that is consecutive happens one after the other. Cal Ripken Jr. of the Baltimore Orioles played in 2,632 consecutive games.

no-hitters (NO-HIT-turz): No-hitters are games in which a pitcher, or group of pitchers, allows the opposing team no hits. Nolan Ryan pitched more no-hitters than any pitcher in history.

pennant (PEN-unt): A pennant is a flag that is a symbol of a team winning the championship of the American League or National League. In 2009, the New York Yankees won their 40th American League pennant.

postseason (POHST-see-zuhn): The postseason in baseball are the series of games played to determine the champion. The Giants went to the postseason 24 times since beginning play in 1883.

steals (STEELZ): Steals are when a base runner moves to the next base without help from the batter. Rickey Henderson had a single-season record of 130 steals in 1982.

streak (STREEK): A streak is an unbroken series of events. Joe DiMaggio is remembered for his 56-game hitting streak.

strikeout (STRIKE-owt): A strikeout is an out made when a pitcher gets three strikes on a batter. Nolan Ryan set the all-time strikeout record.

LEARN MORE

Books

Bildner, Phil. *The Unforgettable Season: The Story of Joe DiMaggio, Ted Williams and the Record-setting Summer of '41.* New York: G.P. Putnam's Sons, 2011.

Jacobs, Greg. *The Everything Kids' Baseball Book.* Cincinnati, OH: Adams Media, 2010.

Minden, Cecilia, and Marsico, Katie. *Baseball.* Ann Arbor, MI: Cherry Lake, 2009.

Web Sites

Visit our Web site for links about baseball records:
childsworld.com/links

Note to Parents, Teachers, and Librarians:
We routinely verify our Web links to make sure they are safe and active sites. So encourage your readers to check them out!

INDEX

Aaron, Hank, 8, 9, 11
Alexander, Pete, 15
Atlanta Braves, 19, 20, 22
Baltimore Orioles, 5, 20
Blyleven, Bert, 17
Bonds, Barry, 8, 9
Boston Red Sox, 21, 29
Brock, Lou, 12
Buhner, Jay, 23
Cadore, Leon, 24
Carlton, Steve, 17
Chesbro, Jack, 15
Chicago Cubs, 22, 23
Chicago White Sox, 6, 21
Cincinnati Red Stockings, 4
Cincinnati Reds, 10
Clemens, Roger, 17
Cleveland Indians, 6, 22
Cobb, Ty, 11, 12
Coleman, Vince, 12, 13
Costantino, Damian, 7
Cox, Bobby, 26
Detroit Tigers, 15
DiMaggio, Joe, 4, 6, 7
Dotel, Octavio, 24
Drysdale, Don, 6
Franco, John, 19
Gagne, Eric, 18
Galvin, Pud, 15
Gehrig, Lou, 5
Griffey Jr., Ken, 23
Hamilton, Billy, 12
Henderson, Rickey, 12
Hershiser, Orel, 6

Hoffman, Trevor, 18, 19
Jackson, Reggie, 28
Johnson, Randy, 16, 17
Johnson, Walter, 15
Keeler, Willie, 6
Koufax, Sandy, 16
LaRussa, Tony, 26
Los Angeles Dodgers, 6, 20, 21
Mack, Connie, 26
Maris, Roger, 8
Mathewson, Christy, 15
Mays, Willie, 9
McGraw, John, 26
McGuire, Deacon, 24
McGwire, Mark, 8
McLain, Denny, 15
Montreal Expos, 10
Morgan, Mike, 24
Musial, Stan, 11
Myers, Randy, 18
New York Mets, 29
New York Yankees, 4, 5, 18, 20, 21, 22, 28
Oakland Athletics, 21, 23
O'Doul, Lefty, 10
Oeschger, Joe, 24
Paciorek, John, 26
Philadelphia Phillies, 10
Pierre, Juan, 12
Pittsburgh Pirates, 22
Pujols, Albert, 9, 28
Radbourn, Charles, 15
Raines, Tim, 12

Ripken, Cal, Jr., 5
Rivera, Mariano, 18, 19
Rodriguez, Alex, 9
Rodriguez, Francisco, 18
Rose, Pete, 6, 10, 11
Ruth, Babe, 8, 9, 28
Ryan, Nolan, 16, 17
St. Louis Cardinals, 9, 13, 20, 21, 29
San Francisco Giants, 8, 20, 21, 22
Seattle Mariners, 22, 23
Simmons, Al, 10
Sisler, George, 10
Smith, Lee, 19
Smoltz, John, 18, 19
Sosa, Sammy, 8
Speaker, Tris, 11
Stairs, Matt, 24
Suzuki, Ichiro, 10
Terry, Bill, 10
Texas Rangers, 29
Thigpen, Bobby, 18
Toronto Blue Jays, 20
Torre, Joe, 26
Ventura, Robin, 7
Villone, Ron, 24
Wagner, Billy, 19
Whitt, Ernie, 20
Wood, Kerry, 17
World Series, 6, 9, 20, 21, 28, 29
Young, Cy, 14, 15